Danielle Steel is a descendant of the Löwenbräu beer barons. Her mother is Portuguese and her father is German. Their common language is French, although they all speak eight languages. Danielle's father's family, the prominent banking and brewing clan, has always lived in Munich and the family seat was a moated castle in Bavaria, Kaltenberg. Her mother's family were diplomats and her maternal grandfather was a Portuguese diplomat assigned to the United States for a number of years.

American-born, Danielle lived in Paris for most of her childhood. At the age of 20 she went to New York and started working for 'Supergirls', a before-its-time public relations firm run by women who organized parties for Wall Street brokerage houses and designed PR campaigns for major firms. When the recession hit, the firm went out of business and Danielle 'retired' to write her first book, *Going Home*.

Danielle has established herself as a writer of extraordinary scope. She has set her various novels all over the world, from China to New York to San Francisco, in time-frames spanning 1860 to the present. She has received critical acclaim for her elaborate plots and meticulous research, and has brought vividly to life a broad range of very different characters.

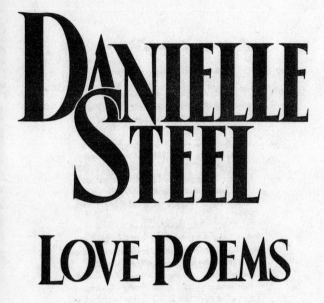

DANIELLE STEEL

LOVE POEMS

WARNER BOOKS

A *Warner* Book

First published in Great Britain by
Sphere Books Limited 1982
27 Wrights Lane, London W8 5TZ
Reprinted 1982, 1983 (twice), 1984, 1985, 1986, 1987, 1988, 1989
Reprinted by Warner Books 1994

Some of the poems in this book appeared
in *Cosmopolitan*, *The Paraclete*, *McCall's*,
Ladies Home Journal and *Good Housekeeping*

Printed in England by Clays Ltd, St Ives plc

ISBN 0 7515 0548 X

Warner Books
A Division of
Little, Brown and Company (UK)
Brettenham House
Lancaster Place
London WC2E 7EN

This is a special book about special people. People who have loved me, and whom I have loved. People who have brought me joy beyond measure, and sometimes incredible pain. People I have hurt, sometimes more than I can bear to think about. People who have hurt me, sometimes more than they know. Yet each of their gifts has been precious, each moment treasured, each face, each smile, each victory, each defeat, woven into the fiber of my being. In retrospect, all of it is beautiful, because we cared so much. In essence, this book covers fifteen years of my life, and a handful of precious people who mean, and have meant, everything to me. This book is written for them.

But in writing this book, or rather putting together the pieces and poems of so many years of my life, I must also thank the many people who have cheered it on, who have written and asked and encouraged and urged this to happen. To all of you, and especially Anne Lerch, my thanks.

And to Linda Grey and Sandi Gelles-Cole, my thanks for a birthday gift beyond measure.

With much love, d.s.

Contents

1

When Love Is New

—*First Meeting*—

Razzle
  dazzle
    snow scene,
my life
  so white
    so bare
      so vast,
and then
  your open
    door,
my heart
  whooshing
    toward
your arms,
  racing
    much
      too fast,
too free,
  as your eyes
waltzed
  slowly
    over me,

the cadence
    yours,
the tempo
    mine,
the music
    poured
        like
            vintage
                wine,
the magic
    of our moment
        so rare,
            so good,
                so new,
as breathlessly,
    I gazed
        at you.

Strangers

Fragments
  of two
    lives
sifted
  through
    fine wire,
spread out
  like
    fans,
added
  and
    subtracted
and shaken up
  like dice,
then rolled
  across
    a board,
     a map,
your life
  laid
    gently
     out

before
   me,
mine
   tossed
helter
   skelter
in your
   lap.

Waiting for Your Call

Backing
 and sidling
hurting
 ribs
 within
 my stall,
fighting,
 fleeing,
 running,
 seeing,
hoping,
 dying,
 aching,
 being,
waiting
 for
the soft
 ring
 of your
 call.

Poem to *Danny*

It doesn't matter
   at all
      if you
         call,
if you care,
   if you dare,
if you
   dream,
if
   you sing
      in a tree.
It doesn't matter
   at all,
      not at all
         ...just
            to me.

Shuffled Papers

Clumsily,
  but gently,
I push
  you
    from
      my head,
as I fumble
  at my desk,
shuffle
  papers,
try to see
  and think
    and do,
when all
  I find
    beneath
      my hand,
        my eye,
my heart,
  is
    you.

No Choice

Comfortable
  in my ivory tower,
barren,
  lonely,
    safe,
hidden,
  shrunken,
    tiny,
      small,
and then you,
  suddenly
    peeking
      over my wall,
with firelit eyes
  and dazzling smile,
I flew away,
  I ran a mile,
I hid from you,
  I shoved you back,
    and then you called,
I felt
  my lack,
    my ache,

your eyes,
　　your smile,
I turned again,
　I ran a mile,
feeling all
　your charms,
hungering
　for your arms,
wondering if
　I'd come
　　to harm
or safe,
　listening for
　　your voice...
knowing that I had
　no choice.

El Señor

You take a matador stance,
   I see you do it,
standing very near,
   you let me brush by,
tucking in your soul,
   looking very whole
     and strong and free,
yet never touching,
   reaching out to me,
    but always there,
you carry fire and smiles
   like darts and banners,
your manner
   pulls me closer,
    I brush near once again,
rushing through your cape,
   you smile,
    you watch,
      you know,
       you wait,
and I fly on and on
   again,
    ever closer,

ever faster,
ever more,
and ever farther
from the safety
of the gate.

Your Call

I wait now
   every morning,
     every day,
       for your voice,
your call,
   your smile,
     your hand,
       your eyes...
waiting for the phone
   to ring,
I realize
   how hard
     I hope
for a reason,
   an excuse,
     a word,
       a game,
an anything,
   a joke,
     a song,
       a ring...
I wait
   and then

I hear
your voice
at last...
I smile...
I fly,
I sing!

Party Shoes

Brown galoshes
and red party shoes,
my old life
and my new,
my days alone,
my life with you,
funny funky
old galoshes,
sad and brown and cold,
then you, my love,
smiling, sparkling,
shy yet bold,
changing my life,
my world,
my blues,
to dazzling,
dancing,
party shoes

—Zippety Click—
I Love You

Zippety click,
   hop and skip
     from one thing
      to another,
dancing,
   running,
having one sweet
   hell of a good
    time,
zippety click,
   involvement
all those
   lovely causes
    to espouse,
and people
   to be met,
until quite
   suddenly
    today,

everything
 went Pow!
I love you,
 can you even
  start
   to think
of such a silly
 joke
  today?
I love you,
 by golly,
  yes,
   I do.
I do love you
 today.

From Opposite Ends

From opposite ends
  of the earth
    we came,
trundling
  our bags,
    our treasures,
our laughter,
  our
    hearts.
From opposite ends
  of the city
    we came,
from different points
  where we
    once stood,
so near,
  yet far apart.
From opposite ends
  of the world
    we came,

silent and cautious,
   unseen.
From opposite ends
   of a lifetime
      we came,
and found
   a breath
      of magic
         hovering
            in between.
From opposite ends
   of a kiss
      we come,
to hold
   each other
      tight
         beneath
            a starry sky.
From opposite ends
   of a heart
      we smile,
two lives
   blended
      into one,
with no more
   opposites
      to approach,

but simply together,
   laughing
      and young,
the beautiful man
    that you are,
      and I.

—Each of Us—

Each of us
  with our
    secret gifts,
magic potions,
  lovely notions,
    waiting to be
      shared,
waiting to be
  aired,
each of us
a half,
a whole,
  a mind,
    a soul,
      a heart,
and yet
  a part
of a better
  richer
    more,
      looking for the
door,
  the key,

the you,
the me,
the we
growing
day by day,
looking
for the way
to find
what
I'd always
dreamed
and never seen,
always tried
and never been,
always thought
but never knew,
until at last
I discovered
that the gift
I always sought
was you.

Knots

The rest
  of the world
    sits
      around
        in a knot,
a complicated
  ball
    of strangled
      confusion
and bungled
  hopes
    beyond
      repair.
While we
  in simple
    silence
have our
  private
    miracle
      to share.
O pity
  the poor
    tangled,

strangled
knots,
which we,
thank God,
are
not!

Are You Comfortable?

Are you
    comfortable?
Can you
    breathe?
Two pillows
    or one?
Is my arm
    crushing
      yours?
Is your
    leg
      wedged
        too tight
          under mine?
Are my hipbones
    too pointy?
      My nipples
      too
        small?
Oh, stranger

asleep
　　at my side
　　here
　　　　tonight,
are you
　　warm?
　　Am I
　　　　safe?
Could you
　　love me
　　　　at all?

—Daughter of— Love

I've never laughed
   when I made
      love
         before,
never touched
   tenderly
      and kissed,
feeling
   young
      and old,
and then
   rolled
      over
         slowly
with a smile
   of glee,
as looking up,
   you kiss
      my eyes,
and say

something
   silly,
      teasing
         me.
I never knew
   that a bed
      was
         a place,
where
   people
      shared
         their hearts
            with smiles.
I never
   made love
      with
         a giggle
            before,
laughing
   and glowing,
and silently
   knowing
that
   laughter
      is part
         of the art,

like hands
    are to gloves....
I just never knew
    that laughter
        was sweet
and so much
    a daughter
        of love.

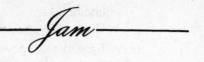
Jam

Jam.
  There must be jam,
    you told me
      firmly,
with a half-hidden
    smile
      of satisfaction
and a promise
    I was yet
      to understand.
You were making
    your presence known.
Toast.
  Eggs perhaps.
    Double coffee,
      some milk,
        one sugar,
maybe juice,
    but always,
      always
        jam.
Yes, I understand.
    I think I can

manage
that,
monsieur,
even in my halfstate
in the morning
And you sat
watching
with the smile
that made me feel,
so bright, so gay,
so light...
and then I knew
you'd spend
the night....
You did, my love,
and there was
breakfast
in the morning,
with birds
singing,
hearts flying,
sun streaming
in over scrambled eggs,
and ham...
and, oh, yes,
of course...
there was jam.

— Nary a Care —

You're gone,
   new lover.
Gone
   to your day,
      to your life,
         to your way
            of doing things,
whatever it is
   you do,
      when you are far
         from me.
And I,
   like a child
      with a dream,
gaze
   starry-eyed
      into the summer
         rain,
feeling anguish,
   gentle
      pain,
fearing
   you will vanish

from the bright
universe
we created
side by side
last night.
And then,
in bittersweet
despair,
I linger
with a cup of tea,
fearing
you have forgotten me,
feeling foolish,
old with fright,
yet young
with promise
long forgotten
in my distant
dreams....
And suddenly,
you're at
the door,
full of brand-new
schemes
for this path
we choose
to share.

Home from your wars,
    from your tasks,
        from your day,
            with nary a care
and only more love
    to strew
        on my way.
I rush
    to your arms
with a gurgle
    of laughter,
        a thunder
            of glee.
Dream man
    come true,
you actually
    did
        come back
            to me!

Moonlit Sunshine

What
do you
do
for me
with me
to me?
You
send
silver
sparkle
thunder
moonlit
sunshine
shivers
through
and through
and through
me.

2

Growing Together

Sunshine
Dancing

Heavenly, heavenly
  mornings
      unraveling
        our bodies
and then tying them
    in a fresh knot
      with sleepy smiles
          and tender words,
as morning birds
    sing past our window,
        sunshine dancing
          on our life,
and I for the first time
    ever
        feeling like
          a wife,
yet lover, friend,
      making breakfast,
        smiling to myself
as I burn the toast,
      and break the eggs,

still feeling
   your hands
      and kisses
         on my legs...
surely this is what
   life
      always had in store...
oh, darling,
   you make me ache for you,
      always hungry,
         always glad,
            always wanting more...

Ordinary
Pleasures

I love our mornings,
 waking,
  finding you there
   next to me,
    smiling,
desperately needing
 that first cigarette
  to start your day,
and then dashing off
 to make you eggs,
seeing visions of
 your face,
  your hands,
   your legs,
your back
 as I juggle coffee,
  butter toast,
and wonder what
 I love the most
  about all that it is
   you are,

brightest star
   in my heavens,
      answer to all my
         unborn dreams
           and secret wishes,
I clatter dishes and
  arrive
     to help you undress
        after you have just put
         yourself together,
the weather is sublime
  and we are fine,
and you are more precious
  than you know,
     as we both begin to
     glow,
it is another perfect day...
   and then you're on your way
    to work
      and I, wife-style,
       driving,
thriving on the rich
  delights
   we share,
the tiny ordinary pleasures,
  I come home

and tuck into my heart
like wondrous
sparkling
tiny treasures.

Friend

My house
   my car
      my bed
         my arms
my life
   my soul
      my smiles
         and all
            my dreams
are touched
   by the magic
      of your
         sounds,
your
   smell,
the perfume
   of your life
intertwined
   with mine
      in a silvery
         blend,
so that I can

think
of only
you,
precious
lover,
partner,
friend.

Comfortable

You shout at me
  and I yell
    back,
you push,
  I shove,
and we squabble
  comfortably
over who sleeps
  where,
which side,
  whose spot,
you are,
  I'm not,
you won't,
  I will,
you grouse,
  I'm shrill,
a symphony
  of loving,
a song
  for every day,
a way

to say
"I love you"
in our own
familiar way.

Bill

I love your macho swagger,
  the look in your eye,
    in your smile,
      all the while
        you move toward me.
You always seem to know
  I'm there,
sometimes I sit back
  and stare
    quietly
      for a while,
waiting for you to know
  I'm near.
You sense it,
  see me,
and walk purposefully
  toward where I wait,
as I fall in love
  with you again,
watching your special
  just you
    macho
      gait.

Rainbow Dreams

As evening comes,
  I race,
already hungry
  for your face,
    your hand,
      your touch,
so much you have
  to give,
    and lavish on me
      with such style...
I think of you...
  I see you smile...
my heart dances,
  prances,
    runs, cavorts,
      and preens,
as quickly
  I do my face,
    my hair,
      and wait for you,
        with a myriad
of rainbow dreams.

—Ball of Yarn—

I have this funny
   ball of yarn
      in the corner
         of my head.
It sits there
   nice and neat
      and then I walk over,
         pick it up,
            look at it,
smile,
   and then I start
      to worry it
         a little,
just because it's
   there,
and then it starts
   to look all
      tangled up
         and messy
and I start
   to trip
      and fall
         in my ball of yarn.

Then you come home
and gently
pluck it
from my hands,
smooth it out
and make it
neat
again,
set it down,
and smile at it
with me
and I know
again
why I'm so glad
when you come home.

Zigzag

Dashing
 zigzag
across
 the pattern
  of our life,
playing
 husband,
  mother,
   genius,
    wife,
scholar,
 chauffeur,
  student,
friend,
 then finding
you alone,
 for a fraction
of a moment,
 a sliver
  of a day,
loving
 what you are

and wish
    and try to be
in a very
    very
        special
        way.

Love's Tango

In an anthill,
  in a tree,
    in a crowd
      of sixty-three,
I feel
  lost
    and then
      confused,
but smile
  at you,
    bemused,
you squeeze
  my hand,
    we swim
      for land,
you hold
  my arm
and render
  harm
    a useless thing,
      a broken
        spear.

With you,
  my love,
    I know
      no fear.
Only
  warmth
    and sunny skies
that dance
  love's
    tango
      in
        your eyes.

Cool

Okay,
  okay
    so
      I'll be
        cool.
At least
  I can
    pretend
      to be,
since
  you can't
    see
      me
near
  the phone,
    or lying
      in the bath
        at night,
wondering
  if
    you'll
      marry
        me.

3

Growing Apart

Peeling Away

I feel you
  peeling
away
  from
    me,
like sticking
  plaster
    tearing
      slowly
from a wound,
  a layer
of my skin
  soldered
    to yours
      until
suddenly
  slowly
infinitely
  painfully,
you began

to pull,
just
    a little
        not
            a lot,
just enough
    to make me
        wonder,
and then
    suddenly
all of it
    being torn
        asunder,
my heart
    with its
        top
            popped,
drunk
    emptied,
        finished,
            gone,
                and now the
rest
    of me
        pried
            loose,
                torn free,

and I tired,
          frightened,
               crying,
                    wondering
                         why
you can't
     love
          me.

Recapture
the Dream

I want to come back
  to you,
want to feel happy
  about you again,
I want to look up
  at your eyes
    and giggle with glee,
not see
  the reflection
    of the pain you've caused me.
I want to feel merry
  and good,
and grateful for your love,
  not distant and remote
    and somewhere
      far
        above.
I want to fly
  to your arms
    like a child

sailing
off
a swing.
I want to remember
the warmth
your loving can bring.
I'm so tired
of the chill,
the winter,
the snow.
Can't we rekindle
the fires,
and bring back the glow?
So much between us,
So much sorrow
it would seem...
oh, distant man,
help me
recapture
the dream.

Trying to Pretend

Trying
  to pretend
    I'm cool,
lying
  in the bed
that is
  absolutely
    vast
      without you.
Trying to pretend
  that I
    don't
      care
how late
  your key
    plays
      chimes
        in my ear
as it turns
  in the lock.

Trying to pretend
    I'm
        free
but stayed
    home
        only
            because
                it rained
and I
    was tired
        tonight.
Trying to pretend
    that I
        don't
            care
but caring
    far
        too
            much.
Trying to pretend
    that I don't
        give
            a damn
                about you,
my one
    and only
        man.

So go out.
  Go ahead.
Don't come home.
  Stay out.
    Get drunk.
      Get laid.
        Fly free.
I'll be here
  all night tonight,
trying to pretend
  I am
    the super splendid
      lady cool
I can't
  even
    begin
      to pretend
        to be.

Regret

Someday I will learn,
　I will stand stately,
　　proud,
　　　noble, dear,
　　　　as you expect.
And reluctantly
　relinquish
　　the unpredictable,
uncontrollable child
　you have known.
That look of dark despair,
　of fear,
suspicion,
　of "oh...what now?"
　　that you glaze me with
　　in darker hours.
Fierce frown,
　flashing eyes,
brows so tightly knit,
　they bristle
　　to discourage
　　　girlish prattle,

that prattle is the last shout
   of those baby days
      you long to know.
Sometimes mere girlish glee,
   harmless,
      yet unwanted.
Someday it will fade
   slowly, unnoticed.
Till it is gone,
   and I will have become
      the woman,
         and not the girl.
The girl will vanish
   if you wish it so.
Will you be proud?
   I don't believe you will.
Too late, my love,
   too late,
      and we shall share
         Regret.

Peekaboo

You run
  in and out
    of my simple
      life,
as though
  it were
    a game,
a child's sport,
  a sort of
    forest
where you can
  dart
    among
      the trees.
Now I see
  you,
    now I
      don't.
Perhaps you
  will,
    perhaps
      you won't.

The phone lies
    still.
It means
    you're happy
        somewhere
            else.
The phone
    then comes
        alive again.
It means
    you're tired
        of the world
            of men.
You come,
    you go,
        you flit,
            you fly,
You run into
    my arms,
you lie.
    You disappear.
And then I see
    you,
        standing there,
playing
    peekaboo

behind
   a tree.
Oh, no.
   No more.
This time
   I score.
Farewell,
   poor childish man.
      Have your fun.
         Live your life.
            Play all your games.
         But not
            with me.

Lies

Where do you go
  when you go out
    for milk
      and come back
        seven hours later?
What happens
  when you park
    the car
      and go home
        somewhere else?
Whose cigarettes
  are you buying
    when you go out
      for mine
and come back
  with the wrong brand?
Whose name do you
  mutter
    in your sleep?
What heart do you
  keep
    in your pocket,
      hidden from my eyes?

What lies will you
    concoct next,
        my dear,
while I pretend
    that I don't fear
        the end
which came so long ago
    while I pretended
        not to hear
its deathlike
    footstep
        on my heart?

Noise

Motorcycle,
    airplane
        noises,
hot rock
    on the stereo
        in your car,
swift step
    and static
        always
            in the air.
Ever quicker
    pace
        hastening
            away ·
from peace
    toward
        noise,
playing
    volleyball
        amidst
            the people
                in your life.

Run faster
    faster
        still
midst
    your self-created
        noise
that will never
    kill
        the angry
            whispers
                of your soul.

Cold

A thousand dreams
   we shared,
     a thousand tears
      we shed,
a thousand days,
   a thousand nights,
     a thousand joys,
      a thousand fights,
a thousand episodes,
   a thousand epithets,
     a thousand hopes
      you shattered
       at my feet,
a thousand hearts
   you scattered
     and then mine,
and all the time
   I thought
     you cared,
how rare
   the joke,
     how sweet the gag,

how much I thought
   you loved
     this hag
a thousand years
   ago,
     my dear,
a thousand moments
  strung like tears,
    icicles across
      my soul,
a thousand ways
  of letting love,
    once oh so warm,
     die softly,
and then grow
  very
    very
      cold.

Only Violets

Only violets,
  I only wanted
    violets,
not masses of
  red roses,
    and vulgar ribbons,
      and finery,
        and lies.
I only wanted
  violets,
just two
  or three,
    or scribbles
      in the sand,
a trinket,
  some small
    thought,
a warm hand
  in the rain,
a smile,
  an apple,
    or some trifling

imperfection
         I could love.
Too much,
    and much too little.
A turtle,
     yes, a turtle
         would be nice too,
three-leaf clovers
    and fading leaves,
not stifling vulgarity
    and expensive emptiness.
But now I know how
    costly are the trifles,
how dear
    and almost
         unattainable.
Just violets,
    my love,
just that,
    remember it
         next year.

Carved
in Stone

You carve me
  in stone now
with your
  lazy
    finger
      sculpting
        me,
etching
  the icy
    nooks
you once made
  soft
    and warm,
you carve me
  in stone
    now
with the plastic
  passion
    of your
      torch,

shooting
   tinfoil
      sparks
         at my flinching
            marble.
You carved me
   differently
      before,
turned
   my wood
      to bark,
         bearing leaves,
giving birth
   to flowers
with the powers
   of your
      burning
      love,
which secretly,
   we both know
      burns
         no
            more,
as your lukewarm,
   too weak,
      too quick
         to chill,

fraying magic
  forces me
    to speak,
when once
  silence
    was
      enough.
Now,
  after you are
    rough,
you ask
  "happy?"
    just before
      you go,
and silently
  I nod
    my head,
whispering
  softly
    "no."

Dread

I dread you
    now,
dread
    your touch
and the smile
    that doesn't
        warm
            me
                anymore.
I dread you
    now,
your hand
    that frightens,
        makes me
            flinch
and hurts me
    to
        the
            core.
I dread
    you
        now,

your anger
quicker
than
the laughter
that
we
knew.
I dread you
now,
dread
the sight
of all
that
I
no longer
see
in
you.

Nothingness

A man
  touched me
    today,
and covered me
  with
    nothing,
a man
  I used to
    love,
the one
  I cared
    about
      so much,
but this time
  as he
    touched me
      with his nothingness,
there was only
  shock
    to realize
how far
  behind
    I'd left
      him.

The Year of the Bears

Side by side
   through the winter,
     tucked in
      like bears,
we snuggled
   and hugged
   and shared
    all our cares,
we teased
   and we talked,
and we whispered
   a lot,
until suddenly
   spring
    and at once
     you were
      not...
not mine
   and not there,
not here
   and nowhere,

your eyes
        empty
            in mine,
your lies
    never
        on time,
until finally,
    grieving,
I knew
    from your trend,
that our
    magical,
        mystical,
            marvelous
year of the bears
    had come
        to
            an
                end.

Desperation

In desperation
   I counted
      on my fingers
         whom to call,
to turn to,
   reach out for,
      cling to.
Seven, eight,
   nine
      people
         to hold
            close...
nine,
   seven,
      four,
         none.
Mistaken
   I had been
      in desperation,

finding that
    others wouldn't
        do.
I only
    wanted
        him.

I Go

I can't bear it
  anymore,
    I can't...
too much anger,
  too much pain,
    too much sorrow,
     too much rain,
no matter how madly
  we once
    loved
     each other,
I can't trudge
  another
   step
on this lonely
  journey
    by myself...
left here
  on the shelf
where you put me
  for safekeeping,
I sit here,
  always weeping,
   waiting

for your return,
while deep inside
   I burn
      with slow despair...
I care...
   oh, darling,
      yes, I care...
but now I can't,
   I won't,
I will not sit here
   dying,
      fading,
         crying,
loving,
   hating,
      waiting
         for the fates
to deposit you
   in my arms
      once more
with your smile
   so rich and slow...
oh, no, my love,
   I can't
      love you or not,
         this time...
            I go.

Silence on the Stair

I watch
   the top
     of his head
as he travels
   quickly
     downward
into the vortex
   of the spiral
     staircase,
running
   down,
lightly
   like water
     down a mountainside,
his feet
   barely touching
     one step
before they rush
   headlong
     toward
       another...

he waves
   his hand,
      then looks
         up,
sunlight
   dancing
      on his face.
It is
   a moment
      filled
         with grace...
and then
   despair.
Before
   I gave
      my heart
         its head
to tell
   its tale,
I let him
   go,
I let him
   flee,
to dance
   his freedom
      dance
         so far from me.

Gone now.
Gone.
And only
silence
on the
stair.

4

Letting Go

Free

Setting the bird free,
   raven haired,
     soaring high above my head,
watching him,
   wings stretched out,
with only a brief last look
   back,
circling high,
   wider now,
pride swooping low
   in my heart,
and coursing through
   my veins,
pride
   because I set him
     free,
only to remember
   all too quickly
     that it was not
       I,
     but he,
and with a last tender
     look

at my now empty
    horizon,
I know that he was
    always
        free.
Gone now,
    raven bird,
        gone to your own sun,
far from mine,
    far from here now,
much beloved bird,
    fly well,
        soar high,
            go free.

Bereft

What is it like for you right now?
  Is the snow as grayish
    as the world you left behind?
Is it all as filled
  with being busy,
is it as much effort
  to laugh harder than the crowd?
Have you told as many
  funny stories?
Have you almost cried
  as many times?
Or are you really having fun,
  the very best of times,
and feeling much relieved
  to be cavorting
    in the snow,
and very far away at last,
  feeling that you have
    escaped
before the time could come
  when people don't turn back?
Or worse,

have you just forgotten
everything that passed?
Are you being happy?
Or feeling quite bereft
the way I do?

Crash into My Life

Did you mean
　　to crash
　　　　into my life
　　　　　this way,
leaving everything
　　so topsy-turvy
　　　as you left?
Do you mean
　　to tell me
　　　that you
　　　　　didn't know
　　　　　　I'd care?
Did you really
　　think I'd laugh
　　　and walk
　　　　away?
How small you must have
　　thought me,
if even
　　for a moment
　　　you believed

I could
    smell roses
      in the air
and taste
    champagne
      again,
and walk
    away
      at midnight
to rake
    my leaves
      and give up
        life again.

If I Can

How do I find my way back
   from the place
     where you
      led me?
The arbor,
   the swing,
     the lilac,
      the ring,
the promises, the dawn,
   the dreams
     that they spawned.
I understand.
   It is all different now,
     you aren't a boy,
      you're a man.
But show me, my love,
   the way back
     from it all,
and I'll follow the path
   if I can.

Sketch

That sketch of you
   so perfect
      at the time,
so endearing
   because you smiled
      above it
as we stared at it
   together,
      pleased.
Now it stares
   at me,
      alone,
and hangs coldly
   on my wall,
no longer part
   of you,
      or us,
no longer anyone
   I even
      once
         remotely knew.

It is but
    a strong man's
        face,
your kind
    of eyes.
A man
    in a beret.
Someone
    born here
        on my wall.
It could be
    anyone
        but you,
in fact
    it is
        no one
            at all.

Fingering Our Sand

Going back
　　to tender places,
　　　full of you,
touching
　　once warm
　　　moments,
　　　　looking at
our sun,
　　standing
　　　twixt
　　　　our sea
　　　　　and sky,
and fingering
　　our sand,
　　　looking at
　　　　the places
we both
　　once wore
　　　like hats,

I wondered where
    the moments
        went,
flying past
    my head
like cranes
    and darting
        through
            my feet
                like rats.

Silence

Your silence hurts,
  it weighs heavily,
    dammit,
I cared so bloody much,
  I hurt, I gave,
    I cried,
      I wanted,
needed,
  hoped,
    the scope
      of it all
        still overwhelms me
as I paint portraits
  in the sky,
    seeing you
      in my life's eye,
        painting in
your presence
  for a thousand years
    to come,
wanting, wishing,
  hoping,
    seeing,

yet frightened
   that
      you'll
         fade away...
and then,
   trembling,
      I realize
         once more...
there was no call
   from you
      today.

No One There

I offer him
  silence
    and take back
      despair.
I look
  for a rainbow
    and find
      only dust.
I wish
  for a dream
    and wake up
      in a trance.
I cling
  to a smile
    and choke
      on a sob.
I tender
  my hand
    and bring back
      the air.

I reach
for the man
and find
no one
there.

Soaring
Silver Bird

Soaring silver bird
  in the noonday
    sky,
weighted
  with the man
    who chose
      to leave me.
I wish
  for safety,
pray
  for flame,
knowing hotly,
  in the midst
    of my confusion
      that
        flame
or no
  he will be
    dead
      to me
        now.

Fear Not ——
Farewell

Fear not,
　　sweet love,
the hands
　　of time,
for poems
　　do not
　　　　always
　　　　　　rhyme,
fate runs
　　its course
　　　　and plays
　　　　　　its tricks
and in the
　　last
　　　　and final
　　　　　　mix,
one wins
　　it
　　　　all
　　　　　　and loses
　　　　　　　naught,

if love
   was good
      and battles
         fought
to their
   very
      final
         end,
good-bye,
   sweet love,
farewell,
   my friend.

Fragile Moments

Shock.
  Blast.
    Zap.
      Gone.
Gone?
  Gone.
    He's gone
      now.
Dead.
  Finished.
    Over.
Yes,
  gone.
And strange
  how it
    all works,
      how it
happens,
  what lasts
    in one's
      mind.

Only the
    tiny
        fragile
            moments,
                the unlikely
gems,
    the morsels,
    and not
        the cake,
the taste
    of the whole
        forgotten,
and only
    the faint
        perfume
            of unreality
                remains...
his whims...
    his smile,
        the guileless
            way he looked
only once
    or twice,
        and in a thrice
            he's gone,

the tale
   too brief
     to tell,
and you remember
   nothing
      very long
         or
            very well.

5

Lonely Feelings

Couples

Couples.
  Happy couples,
clinging close,
  hugging tight,
    dancing fast,
      being one,
laughing loud,
  singing high,
    giggling shrill,
      showing off,
loving love,
  living hard,
    and making
      my heart
break
  and
    snap
      and
die
  as
    I
      watch
        them

from
this
spot
where
I
still
stand
alone.

Two Thirds

Two thirds
   and two thirds,
Two apartments,
   two separate
     homes,
       neighbors.
Together
   we make
     four thirds,
one
   too
   much
and twice
   one
    short.
You have
   your
     man,
       neighbor woman,
and I
   my child,
and as your husband

trotted
        down
            the
                stairs
today
    with his dog
        and my child,
            I watched
his legs,
    the sway
        of his hips,
            the way
                his haircut
ended,
    and you watched
        my small girl's
            bright red
                sneakers,
starlit hair
    and tiny hand
clasped
    in his
        larger
            one.

Two thirds
we are
in either
house,
and neither
of us
whole.

Woman Laughing in the Night

Shrilly,
  a voice
    in the night
caw caws
  raven-fashion,
it is a cactus
  sound,
it prickles me,
  and, curious,
    I rise,
stealthily
  pulling back
    lace curtains
that have
  come to me
    too soon.
Silently
  I watch...

a taxi
    giving birth
        to a man,
            and then
                a woman.
She laughs again.
    She gropes
        for him,
throwing back
    her head,
hurling
    laughter
        from her mouth
again
    like sparks
        this time,
            staccato,
                sharp,
he fondles her,
    the cab leaves,
        I watch.
She laughs again
    and he silences
        her,
            but only for an instant,
                with a kiss.

She laughs
   she holds his hand
      she leads him
         home,
her prey
   into her laughter lair.
while I,
   too soon old
      while still
         so young,
watch,
   bereft,
      alone,
         unseen.

On the Riverbank

Two men once
  found
    me
naked
  on the riverbank
    at different
      times,
and then
  a third
    came by.
All brothers,
  all the same,
    seeking
only
  naked
    maidens
near a
  body
    of cool
      water

to quench
   their many
      thirsts.
Two men
   left me
      on that
         riverbank,
the third
   left
      me
         for dead,
and if
   a fourth
      should
         happen
            by,
he'll not
   find me
      on the
         riverbank
listening
   for his
      tread.
He'll find
   me
      armed
         and shielded,

hidden
near
a strong,
stone wall,
if a fourth
should even
happen
to find me
there
at all.

Boat Come In, Tide Go Out

I sat and watched
  a boat
    come in,
the tide
  go out,
a bird
  fly by,
a man
  swim past,
a life
  go by.
The sun
  had set,
the man
  had gone,
the tide
  was out,

the day
   was done,
the life
   gone by
was mine.

—Princes, Toads —

Princes,
   toads,
     and butterflies,
sugar cookies,
   bitter apple tarts,
     and frosty lemonades,
circus tents,
   and puppy dogs,
     and hayrides,
icy midnight
   swimming
     in a lake,
muddy roads,
   woodsy smells,
     fresh grass,
and dandelions,
   and oranges,
     and wine,
faded denims,
   musty silks,
     and faded memories
of princes
   turned
     to toads.

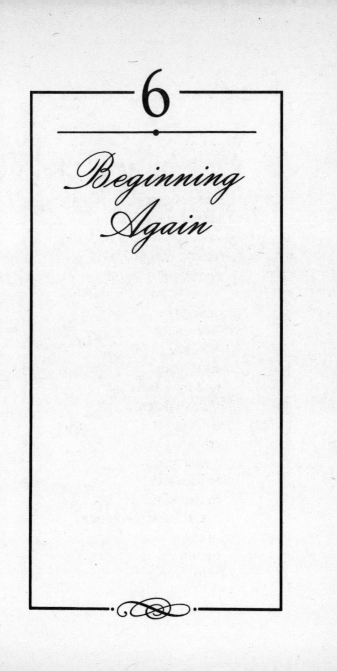

6

Beginning Again

— Now I Want —
the Have

I've faced it then,
  have I?
    I suppose I have.
The magical
  answer
    to the cannonball
    question
"what do you
  really
    want?"
I have want,
  now I want
    the have,
the touch,
  the hand,
    the real,
the feel
  of the same
    leg
cast easily

over mine
    for a decade
        of winter
            mornings...
for two decades...
    or three...
that same leg
    flung
        over
            me,
the same smile.
    A sameness.
Oh, God, yes,
    I'd love that.
I've tasted
    the hors
        d'oeuvres,
nibbled
    at the cakes,
        the pies,
tasted
    all the lies
        of liberty
            and free.
Who sold me
    that?

I want mine
back,
the savage sweet
of same
and same
and same again
the same sweet man
to share
a life
of love
and have and same
with me.

Matador

I play
   a matador's game
     with life,
face it
   squarely,
     deceive
       its sharp
        horns,
wave
   embroidered
     glitter
       in its face,
I flaunt
   who
     I am,
and proudly,
   in the noonday
     sun,
I dance
   for no
     audience,
save
   my own

soul,
I lust not
   for blood,
      merely
         for life.
I stand
   here
      alone,
with the
   cape
      in my hand,
I flee
   not
      from battle,
I laugh
   when
      I can.
Ha! Toro!
   See me here,
      see me
         now!
See me, Life!
   I am
      a Woman!
I am
   no man's
      wife.

Are You — Still There?

Leafing through
   the pages of my address book.
Looking for you,
   your name
      scribbled
        somewhere,
stuffed
   in my back pocket
      lo those many years
        ago.
Groping
   for you
      in the attic
        of my memory,
never
   lost,
      but put away.
Strange time
   to call perhaps,
      your name
        and face

retrieved
  so late
    after time
      has tossed us
both
  from here
    to there.
But now
  I'm here
    again.
      Are you?
Seven numbers
  and a long
    thin
      ring
        ringing on.
You must be
  gone.
    And then your voice
      again.
Surprising
  in its nowness
    right here
      in my room,
as I wonder how
  you look
    these days,

after such a lot
of years
pressed between
the pages
of a frayed
red leather book.

Snow in Your Hair

Snow
   in your
      hair,
         not age,
warmth
   in your
      heart,
         not rage,
a smile
   in your
      eyes
         just for me,
I lean
   gently back
      and you
         are my tree.
Your heart
   has been
      farther
         than mine,

You love
  your cognac,
    your cigars,
      your white wine.
There's no
  haste
    in your
      pace,
you
  no longer
    must
      race,
no more
  do you flee
    or break
      dates,
no need
  to rush
    past,
      dodging fates.
You give me
  the sun
    and the moon
      in your palm,
you need me,
  you love me,

you make me
feel calm.
You gave me
the woman
I wanted
to be,
you hold me
so gently
and let me
feel free,
we stand
close together
and smile
at our truth.
You gave me
the sun,
now I give you
my youth.

Pretend
Forever

Devastating,
  debonair,
    delightful
      man,
and I,
  the dazzling
    darling,
as face to face
  we dance,
    we waltz,
we do a minuet
  of hope
    on our desert isle,
I laugh,
  you smile,
    we float
      with glee,
Together
  hand in hand,
    so free,
then suddenly

I see
     the narrow
          band
of gold
   that holds
      you fast,
         and at last
you see
   that I am
      fettered
         by the same,
and now
   it is
      a kind of game,
         as you hold
            my arm,
I touch
   your sleeve,
      enjoying
         the pretend
            forever
magic
   of our
      cinderella
         eve.

For a Year, For a Day

Music and singing
   and laughter
      and bringing
daffodils
   to toss
      in the air
and nary
   a care,
and a river
   to wear
and a sky
   to put on
      like
         a cloak,
and Coke
   to drink
      and then
         champagne

and carriage
　rides
　　at midnight
　　　in the park,
and all
　a lark
　　until
the gingerbread
　begins
　　to crumble,
and at last
　you stand there,
　　broken,
　　　foolish,
　　　　humble.
Go ahead,
　sing.
　　Don't wait
　　　for a ring.
Laugh
　while you may,
　　for a year,
　　　for a day,
smile,
　and never look
　　harried,

if the man
    you insist
        that you
            love
is
    already
        married.

Peacocks and Frogs

Peacocks
  and frogs.
Princes
  and pickles.
Gingham
  and mustard
    and giggles
      and tickles.
Onions
  and daisies
and raindrops
  and stars.
Cheap wine
  and fine wine
    and love
      sold in jars.

— *Sacred Papers* —

Front page,
  back page,
    sports page
and financial
  section
    all a jumble?...
Oh, no,
  it is
    not I
      who'll make
        you mumble
in despair,
  wondering
    precisely
      where
the page one
  news
    has fled,
as you
  lie
    cozily
      abed,

sipping tea
and smoking
while
exasperatedly
and in secret
choking
wondering
where
in hell
the Dow Jones
might be...
Oh, no...
no sacred
rite
to be
defiled
by me.
Separate
papers,
separate
baths,
united joys
delighted
laughs,
the meeting
of two

very
   independent
      sorts,
while above us
   one big
      bright star
         cavorts
and tall trees
   which gently
      flow and bend,
and in our laps,
   two morning
      papers,
sacred
   till the
      very
         end.

Too Much

Silence today...
     too busy?
        You couldn't
           get through?
What does it mean?
   Are you already bored?
      Does it matter?
         Is the telephone
            out of order?
I check my watch
   again
      and fiddle with
         the border
            on the bed,
running reasons
   through my head,
      thinking
         of all the possibilities,
why perhaps you
   couldn't call
      last night...

but still
  a chill
    of fright....
        Does it matter?
        Has he fled?
And slowly,
  I go back
    to bed,
heavy hearted,
  lonely,
    and a little bit afraid...
Have I played it wrong
  this time?
Too open?
  Too much too soon?
    Or is it something
      that I've said?
Or have I quickly become
  just anyone,
a someone to take
  for granted,
    an old shoe?
Or is it that I am
  already
    much too much
      in love
        with you?

Open Hand

Oh, such an open hand
  I hold out to you,
    so wide open,
      filled with my heart,
my soul,
  my life,
    my sins
      and pleasures
        and despairs.
It used to be
  that I held it all
    hidden
deep inside
  my pockets,
    for none to see,
no one to hurt
  or touch
    or tell,
yet already I know you
  so well,
    trust you so much,
that I hold it all
  out for you to touch

and see...
knowing that
you won't
hurt me,
oh, treasured,
gentle,
much loved man
to whom I hold out
my open hand.

Only Close

Yes, love,
   I know,
     it's hard
       for both of us...
my wanting,
   needing,
     hoping,
       waiting,
almost
   seeming
     to be baiting
as I reach
   out
     in a way
that fills
   you
     with
       fear...
it's
   all right,
     runner man,
it's okay,

yes
   I know
you'll stay
  while
    you can
then you'll
  go
and I'll
  grow,
and I'll
  cry
    for a while...
      ssshhh...
it's all right,
  darling,
    smile.
I shan't
  get you
    lost
      in a life
        that you dread.
as visions
  of wedding rings
    dance
      in your head.
Fear not,
  don't flee.

I only
want you
close
to me.

Fondly

I care about you.
  I like you.
I relate to you.
  I understand you.
I feel for you.
  I'm fond of you.
    You're dear.
Oh, no, my dear.
  You're not even
    here,
nor barely
  there
    with your "fond"
     words
that relate
  to like
    and care.
     You are nowhere.
I need you,
  want you,
    love you.

That's what's
really there,
but do you
dare?

The Inside of Your Arm

You make love to me
  as though
    you wore
      the manual
        on the inside of your arm.
You touch,
  you feel,
  you reel,
you slide
  along the inside
    of my thigh...
      you sigh,
you smile,
  you keep yourself aloof,
    you arch sharply
      toward the roof,
you moan,
  and then you glance
    to see if by chance

I am as transported
    as you want me
        to think you are...
but no,
    no different
        than the backseat of a car
            a century ago,
                and then as well
there's one tiny tender thing
    that you, m'friend,
        forgot
with all your ravishing,
    ravaging,
        macho, sexy, free!...
You never even kissed me.

Good-bye
   hello
      good-bye
         good-bye
hello.
   Hello
      once more.
         Yet again.
And then
   good-bye
   another
thousand
   times
   and
      more.
From
   the end
     to
      the beginning,
and then
   back
    again,

starting
   new,
      no longer
         starting
            fresh,
no
   fresh
      left.
And each
   hello
      has
         the echo
            of good-bye
hidden
   in
      its heart,
ah, yes,
   my friend,
      I know.
         Hello?
Yes.
   For a while.
      And then
         you too
            will
               go?

Twinkles and Sparkles

Twinkles
  and sparkles
    and horrible
      shakes,
shivers
  and giggles
    and frivolous
      quakes.
Vague looks
  and dark looks,
    odd thoughts
      and green eyes.
Yesterday's
  wonders.
    Tomorrow's
      good-byes?

First Hello

First hello
 on a bright
   spring day,
fresh green
 splashed
   on all
     the trees,
flowers
 everywhere,
   in my hair,
our hands,
 your voice,
a ferry boat
 ride,
   laughter,
     songs,
and ice cream
 cones
   on a newly
     painted
       bench.
Then summer
 was ours,

we held it
tight,
grew
brown
and strong
and gay,
sailing days,
and waterfalls,
and woods,
picnics
and promises
and time
always
wanting
to stand
still.
And after
all that,
autumn
came
as a surprise,
crept up,
unfurled
its golden
hair
and scarlet
wares,

it grew chilly,
  leaves fell
    as we began
      to drift,
we had
  no picnics
    left
      to share,
barely time
  it seemed
to remember
  spring
    and salute
      our first
        hello
before
  we said
    our last
      good-bye.

Count

I used
   to count
      my men
but it
   embarrassed
      me,
well
   bred,
      well
         fed,
well
   led
      on a proper
         path
for one
   or two,
perhaps
   secretly
      a third,
         but not
            a fourth.

A fifth?
  Good
    God!
      A sixth,
        disgrace,
and the
  seventh
  could
    only
make
  me know
    I was
      a whore.
Now
  I don't
    count
      my men
ever
  any
    more.

Friend

We compare notes,
  my friend and I...
    shyly, nervously,
      but strangely
willing to tell
  the truth
    about our youth,
      about our then,
        about our now....
How many have you had?
  Did you care
    about them all?
Were they young?
  old?
    splendid?
     tall?
You mean you had one too
  whose name
    you never did
     quite
      know?
All right, all right,
  I understand.

I had one too.
It made me grow.
And a man you clearly
didn't love,
the kind that made
you feel
a whore?...
I had one too...
yes.
What a bore...
and degrading.
It chewed a nibble
from my soul.
Oh, and one so old.
And two so young.
I've come unsprung.
I'm telling you all this?
about them all?
right up to the very end?
But you tell me too,
and I feel good,
loved, accepted,
understood,
sharing my victories
and disgraces,
tragedies
and comedies,

bruises and how they mend…
with one single, very special,
treasured
friend.

7

Love Lost Once More

Sing Softly

Sing softly
  sadly
    hollow
songs
  of bygone
    days
and yearning
  dreams
    of once upon
      an almost time.
Sing gently,
  love,
    at eventide,
on wintry
  nights
    and summer
      days.
Sing to
  your other
    love,
      my love,
and if our time

should come
again,
come softly
to my door
by night.
You'll find me
waiting
for you
there.

Come Back

Funny
   that they all
      come back.
         They always
         do.
Back
   they come
      with a change
      of heart,
long after
   they had
      gone.
Back
   they come
      with all
         the words
            I wanted
once
   to hear.
      But they come
back
   too late.

Ears
go deaf,
hearts
die,
moments
pass
and time
ceases
to be
of much
importance.
This time
make it
different.
Bring him
back
while I
still
care.

—Broken Day—

I bought
  groceries,
    forgot
      to wash
        my hair,
picked up
  a pack
    of cigarettes,
and
  eighteen
    nails,
I had
  a project,
    forgot
      a lunch,
I think
  it rained
    all
      day,
all year,
  all life
    gone
      gray.

Someone
said
that
you
got
married
yesterday.

No Man, Our Man

Was he a man
 the man
  who was
   my man?
You know,
 that man...
  the man...
   my man...
    ...her man.
The man
 who was
  her man,
   was mine,
    I thought,
and I hear
 she thought
  so too.
Foolish
 to think
  the man
   was ours.

No man,
  our man,
    her man,
      my man,
and I only
    wonder
      now and then
        who is his
woman now?

Scoundrel Love

You ask me if I loved the man,
  unworthy as you say he was,
    it seems to me I did,
    my friend,
      without much reason,
        or a good "because."
What a wretch he is now,
  in my ever-clearing brain,
what a dandy, what a scoundrel,
  and, oh, my friend,
  how much pain
    he inflicted on my heart
      without ever looking back.
O alack!
  Plague take the rogue
  and curse his soul,
    what a devil was that man,
    what an evil sort of troll!
But was he really all those things?

Was he quite as vile as that?
Then why is it that I love him,
   sitting here
      and looking back?

He Calls

And now,
  at last,
    he calls,
in tears,
  in fears,
    in dread,
instead
  of having
    loved me
    then.
He calls me
  now,
  in pain,
    in grief,
    in guilt,
with endless sorrow
  for the old cruelties
    he once enjoyed
    so much.
I remember...
  and now
    I answer him
    with caution,

with a sigh...
a distant
something
in my eye,
not quite a tear,
no longer love,
almost anger,
yet
not
quite
hate,
too late...
he asks
if I will see him
and I answer,
cowardly,
vague,
muttering
"don't think I can"
to this
pitiful,
not quite,
too late,
guilty
man.

Octopus
Hectopus

Octopus
  Hectopus
    Hexagon
      Round
        Lovers
who cheat
  make their own
    wailing sound,
shrieking
  like banshees
    explaining their ways,
breaking
  all hearts
    till the end
      of their days.

Someday

Someday
  is a place,
    a time,
      a dream,
a blade of summer
  grass,
    dried out,
and reminiscent
  of a day
    when someday
was reality
  and filled
    with hope.
Someday
  was a word
    we used
      to taunt
        each other,
a distant spot
  we hungered for,
    but were anxious
      not to find
        too soon.

Someday
   was a yearning,
    a man I knew
and loved,
   in a someday
    sort of way,
because today
   was never quite
    his style.
Someday
   was a child
    we would have
    had,
      but didn't,
a time I knew
   would come,
    but never has.

To Clo: Christmas Remembered

The Christmas most dear to me?
  The one we danced beside the
  tree,
  The Christmas you lay next
  to me.
The year we shared each other's
hearts,
  The Christmas we were one.
Ah, dancing man of long ago,
  Come back to me again,
The tree is lit, my stocking's hung,
  I wait now as I have since then,
For but one more Christmas Eve,
  In the brilliance of our midnight
  sun.

Father,
Daughter,
Friend

Extraordinary moments
   stand out now,
special days,
   the big events,
     the times I can't forget...
my wedding day,
   riding in the car
     bathed in a cloud
     of white,
hidden by my veil,
   my hand clutched in yours,
and then you suddenly
   so pale
    as we walked
     up
      the aisle...
and then I smile,
   another time, another day,

while still a child,
wearing something ghastly,
    wild,
and you pretending that
    I looked okay,
        beautiful, in fact,
            divine...
do you remember
    that funny time?
And then the times
    you came to camp,
the day I broke your
    favorite lamp,
the bookcase
    I destroyed,
the absurdity of meeting
    boys,
        and bringing them to you...
the memories a kind
    of glue
        between my then
            and now,
I see you with a furrowed brow
    poring over
        what I wrote,
scribbling, writing,
    making notes,

and in later years,
    only your voice
        in the midnight hours,
as silently I dialed,
    so relieved to find you there,
        so good to know you cared,
how much we said,
    how rich the gifts,
how lucky we both were
    to have been father,
        daughter, friend…
and even now, that you are
    gone,
        the joy of that will never end.

Crying Rainbows

Crying rainbows,
   dripping tears,
      reminding me
         of what you were
         to them,
I listen to your friends,
   I read the notes,
      I nod my head,
         I hold my pen,
I try to say
   the things
      they need
         to hear....
But what of me?
   Where will you be
      next week
         when I'm alone,
or when I want to send
   my book,
      who will look

at my work
the way you did?
Who will speak
the truth,
who will remind me
of my youth?
Must I be a grown-up
now
that you have fled?
Who will tuck me
into bed
if I wish to be
a child again
of one
or two
or three?
Who will take
care
of me
as you used to do?
Oh, Daddy, is it
true
that you are gone,
and I am grown?...
Yes, you are,
I am,

as I sit here,
all alone,
    crying rainbows
  of my own.

8

*And then
you
love again...
carefully
this time.*

Hurray for the Legalized Lover

Were they so wrong
   the madwomen
      of the fifties
who endowed
   each lover
      with the gift
         of wedlock?
Are we so much
   better off
      with bedlock?
Am I so free
   because
      I wear no ring,
and carry only
   my brave name
      after all
         these scars?

Ah, no,
   really,
      I think by now
I ought to
   have a medal
      or two,
a name or three
   or four
      or five.
After all
   is said
      and done
who will know
   that in fact
I was once
   very much
      in love, alive?
And with all
   our lively
      seventies games,
I begin
   to yearn
      for an endless
         fifties
            list of names.

If we're so free
  why should
    we be
      so very undercover?
Next time
  I think
    I'll find me
a name-throwing
  legalized
    lover.

Champagne in My Shoe

Sitting here,
  with early
    morning coffee,
wondering
  where you are
    right now,
I still feel good,
  like well-polished wood,
well-oiled springs,
  waiting to see
    if the morning
      brings
you back,
  or will you wait
    till noon?
      So soon?
Or not until...
  tonight...
    and then a shaft
      of fright...

like sunbeams
at my feet...
so sweet
our hours
before the dawn,
the dreams
they spawned,
the pains
they stilled,
the tears they dried
from years ago,
oh, let it grow
all this bright
new love
I need so much,
your gentle touch
like champagne
in my shoe...
oh, dear new man,
come back,
come back,
I promise I'll be
good
to you....

Over the years,
   I have carried
boxes,
   treasures,
     objects,
       beds,
old shreds
   of people
     who had hurt
      or cared,
people I had pared
   down
     in memories
      and dreams,
people who had shrunk
   and grown,
     those who had left me
     all alone,
I carried them along,
   I sang their song,
I kept their faces
   in sacred places
     in my mind,

a kind of album of my life,
　　my years as child,
　　　my days as wife,
　　　　my broken toys,
　　　　　my shattered joys,
lying in a myriad pieces
　　near my feet,
　　　swept into piles
　　　　with all the smiles
that faded all too soon,
　　as I sat,
　　　woven into the cocoon
　　　　you quietly unwound,
where somewhere
　　deep within
　　　you found me
　　　hidden,
playing with a doll,
　　a bear,
　　　how much I care,
how good you've been
　　as I notice
　　　what I should have seen
　　　　an eternity before...
the debris beneath the bed,
　　the brittle chaos in my head,
　　　the wilted flowers,

forgotten hours,
the whispers and the taste
of ash
buried in the attic
of my not so many years,
and suddenly the tears
seem to have mattered not at all,
it is no longer fall
but spring
as you bring
me all this joy
to have and hold
and keep,
and I,
laughing,
pull aside the blinds,
let in the sun,
hitch up my skirts,
pick up the broom,
and finally,
begin
to sweep.

Brand-new Now

Let us not
  confuse
    the actors
      in the play.
He hurt me,
  she broke
    your heart.
He left me,
  and she was
    a rotten cheat.
Let us instead
  see only
    each other.
You took
  my pencil,
I failed
  to wash
    the tub out,
      dry your razor,
we forgot
  to buy

a loaf of bread
for lunch.
Those are
our only
griefs
to cry for.
So if he
left me
long before
you came along,
I bid him now
adieu,
and if she left
you broken,
I'll help you
to begin anew.
And tomorrow
you'll give
back
my pencil,
I'll dry
your razor,
wash the tub out,
and we will buy
the bread
together,

and start
a solid
you-me-now
life.
Only me
and you.

Loving You

Childlike,
  I hear
    the echoes
      in the halls,
the footfalls
  that never came,
I hear the silence
  in the night,
I taste
  the fright,
and yet,
  I am a grown-up
    now,
      or so they say,
a mesh of gray
  woven into my hair,
    too old to care
      if the footsteps
        ever come again...
and yet,
  last night,
    I felt my heart

listen,
   tremble,
     wait,
fearful
   that I shan't find
     you
       waiting at the gate,
fearful that you'll
   cross
     the fields
       and vanish in the night...
too old
   for this fright,
it should not matter
   quite so much...
and yet
   it does...
     it does...
      you do....
The world
   would be
     my tomb
      again
were it not
   for the joy
     of loving you.

Matching the Pairs

The roof
brought down
around
our ears,
the curtains
wrapped
around our
heads,
all our apples
so carefully
stacked,
so instantly
scattered,
the patter
of every day
halted
as we sat there
suddenly
lame,
suddenly tamed
by life

and anger,
        fear,
            and despair,
dismay,
    as we glared
        from
            opposite
                corners,
throwing rocks
    tossing dreams
like used socks
    somewhere
        behind us
into a place
    we would never
        find
            again,
and then scurrying
    about,
clutching
    our accusations
        in our arms,
the charms of each
    forgotten
        until the magic
            clock
began to chime

the hour...
not quite midnight
yet,
still time,
a moment or two,
in which to run
and dash and hurry,
scurry about
again,
finding the socks,
washing them clean,
asking each other
"what did you mean,"
matching the pairs,
saying "I care,"
and just enough
time
to run
from doom,
and meet once again,
in the heart
of the room,
holding out hope,
baring our souls,
feeling my insides
no longer cold,
but slowly warm,

slowly glad,
slowly good,
slowly new,
and you with that
smile,
the same
much loved
you.

Morning
Friends

Quickly
   I pitter-pattered
    up the stairs,
knowing what I'd see
   as I juggled
    your usual breakfast
     order,
more or less,
   but never did I
    guess
that the scene
   I'd meet
would warm my soul
   and mist my eyes,
    and make me realize
    again
how much I care,
   how good you are,
    how sweet the scene
    I saw,

as I heard her whisper
   gently
      "please,"
seeing my daughter,
   her best doll,
      and her teddy bear
perched
   on your knees,
your sleepy face
   peeking between
      the mob
thronging
   in your arms
      as she held your hand
         and you his paw...
how much I loved
   all that
      I saw.

Joy

Joy
  in the morning,
    in our
dawn,
  in your
    sun,
joy
  in the morning,
being
  two,
    feeling
      one.
Your head
  on my pillow,
    my heart
      in your
        hand.
new life
  in our
    loving,
in our
  own
    magic
      land.

The Gift of Love

Ever hopeful,
  filled with dreams,
    bright new,
      brand-new,
        hopeful schemes,
pastel shades
  and Wedgwood skies,
    first light
      of loving
        in your eyes,
soon to dim
  and then you flee,
    leaving me
      alone
        with me,
the things I fear,
  the things you said
    burning rivers
      in my head,
bereft of all
  we shared,

my soul
  so old,
    so young,
      so bare,
afraid of you,
  of me,
    of life,
      of men...
.until
  the bright new
    dreams
      begin again.
The landscape never
  quite the same,
    eventually
      a different game,
aware at last
  of what I know,
    and think,
      and am,
        and feel,
the gift of love
  at
    long
      last
        real.

9

...and then love is born again.

Tomorrow's Child

Small and warm,
tiny hands reach up
to touch and prod,
small toes stretch
and something deep inside
feels like the ripple
of a giggle,
as our tiny
precious
unborn child
begins
to laugh
and dance
and wiggle.

Moonbeam

How proud I am
    of all you are
        and all you do,
how rich I feel
    when meshed
        with you,
how strong
    I know
        our love to be,
how lovely
    to be us,
        yet free,
and how delicious
    this new gift,
        this moonbeam
            in my soul,
this gift of you,
    this part of me,
how very loved
    our child
        will be.

Come Soon

Waiting for you,
little one,
getting ready
a steady
flow
of rainbows
dancing through
my head,
the single thread,
the constant theme,
the tender dream
of you
in our midst
at last,
the planning
and the hope,
the gingham
and the little boat
we bought you
at a fair...
...oh, yes, we care...

we dream,
  we scheme,
    we wait,
we've found the house,
  the home,
    the room...
now, hurry, child,
  come to these
    waiting arms,
who long for you,
  come home,
    come now,
      come soon....

New Life

Silently, I watch you grow,
   magically planted inside of me...
     But soon I'll set you free,
       sweet soul.
You are so small,
   so big, so young, so old...
     you push so hard
       as though to shove me aside...
and soon my heart
   will open wide
     as the magic of your new life
       is unfurled.
And you push yourself
   into your world.
     Go ahead, little one,
I wait here, to cheer you on....

Arrived!

You have arrived
  and safely,
    long awaited miracle,
precious bundle
  lying in my arms,
your eyes staring
  into mine
    as though asking
what took _me_ so long
  to get here,
and I, laughing
  and crying all at once,
    hold you tighter,
      press you near,
feeling you
  so infinitely dear,
    so mine, so ours,
      sweet gift of joy...
the prince!
  The heir!
    Our baby boy!

The Joy
of You

Yes, she was lovely too,
   your sister...
      she came with tissue paper
translucence,
   all white and pink
     and frail,
like porcelain lit from
   within,
     a child to dress in silks
      and pink ribbons,
so perfect,
   and delicate
     in her beauty...
while you, robust fellow,
   lie here,
     beautiful and rosy cheeked,
bright eyed,
   and looking as though
     you should be
      in a swing,

or chasing puppies,
    counting guppies,
or picking flowers in a field,
    eating candied apples,
or cookies,
    dripping crumbs,
        not sucking on my thumb,
as I eye you once again,
    wondering who you are,
        will be,
if you are like her
    or him
        or me,
if your eyes will be
    brown
        or blue,
and then I laugh again,
    overwhelmed
        by the sheer joy
            of you

— Welcome Home —

I have waited a lifetime for this,
  climbed mountains,
    counted dreams,
schemed and prayed
  and danced
    and would have,
      if I'd had to,
        drunk witches' brew...
I would have done all that,
  beloved babe...
    and more...
      just to have you...
I have waited,
  I have pined,
    sometimes cried,
      and never whined,
in silence and in darkness
  I have often prayed,
I have tried to forget the hoping,
  yet never ceasing to muse
    about this day...
wondering if...

wishing that...
    aching, longing,
and then finally knowing,
   growing,
   glowing,
overwhelmed with joy
  and gratitude...
and now this moment,
  you are here...
you've come at last,
   after waiting all these years...
    second child of my heart,
     sweet babe of my dreams,
holding fast to one finger,
  your eyes locked in mine,
your heart already sewn to my own...
  welcome, my darling...
   welcome at last,
    welcome, sweet babe...
Welcome home.

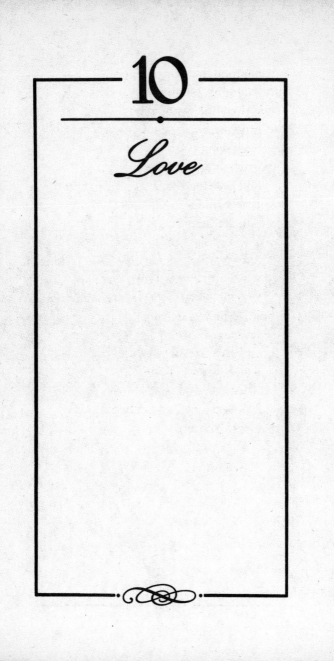

10

Love

Love

Life with its odd endings
   and beginnings,
its occasionally
   very painful
     middles,
its riddles,
   its surprise hellos,
     and at times
      astonishing
      adieus,
its greens, its grays,
   its reds, its blues,
     its flowers which come
like sunbursts
   on a gloomy day,
     given by a man
      you barely know,
and its birthdays
   forgotten
     by the men
      you love...
Life, with its rare gifts,

its strange charm,
its strong arm,
it's vast sass,
its more than occasional
boot in the ass,
its blunt pain,
its bleak rain,
its sorrow
and its grief...
is somehow all too brief,
like a cinderella ball,
so deck the halls,
put on your pumps,
your furs,
your minks,
don't shrink,
put your tiara on,
step out,
prance high,
chin up,
dance nigh
the flame
with eyes aglow,
and above all, dear friends,
before you go,
before it ends,
and there remains

no further tale to tell,
dare once...twice...
often if you choose,
but dare,
yes, dare to love,
and if you do,
make sure that you
love well.
For love is worth it all,
is worth a call,
a dream,
a scheme,
a sleepless night,
a carriage ride,
or crossing
half the world,
for a glimpse, a touch,
a truth...
for love is youth,
is fun,
is grand...
a carnival...
an opera ball....
For truth to tell,
Love is Life...
and Life is Love...
and Love is All.

A very special book from
Danielle Steel

A Perfect Stranger

Tom, the chauffeur, watched Raphaella disappear down the stairs onto the long sandy beach, and then he glimpsed her again as she wandered near where the surf broke. Eventually he could no longer distinguish her from the others, and he climbed back into the car, turned on the radio, and lit a cigarette. By then Raphaella was far down the beach, watching three Labradors chase each other in and out of the water, and a group of young people wearing blankets and blue jeans were drinking wine and playing their guitars.

The sound of their singing followed her further down the beach as she wandered, and at last she sat down on a log and took a deep breath of the salt air. It felt so good to be there, to be out in the world for a few moments, to at least see others living even if she could not do much living herself. She just sat there and watched people passing, arm in arm, kissing, side by side, talking and laughing or jogging past each other. They all seemed to be bent on going somewhere and she wondered where they all went when the sun went down.

It was then that she found herself watching a man who was running. He came from far down the beach in a straight line, running almost like a machine, without stopping, until finally, still moving with the smoothness of a dancer, he slowed to a walk and kept coming down the beach. The fluidity of his movement in the distance had intrigued her, and as he came closer she kept her eyes on him for a long time. She was distracted by a group of children, and when she looked for him again, she saw that he was wearing a red jacket and was very tall, but his features were indistinct until he came closer. Suddenly she gasped. She just sat there staring, startled, unable to move or turn so that he wouldn't see her face. She just sat there watching as Alex came closer and then stopped when his eyes fell on her. He didn't move for a long time, and then slowly, deliberately, he walked toward where she sat. She wanted to run away, to vanish, but after seeing him run down the beach, she knew she didn't have a chance and she had ventured quite far from where she had left the car. Now relentlessly, with his face set, he came toward her, until he stood before her, looking down at her sitting on the log.

Neither of them spoke for a long moment and then, as though in spite of himself, he smiled. "Hello. How are you?" It was difficult to believe they hadn't seen each other in five months. As Raphaella looked up at the face she had seen in her mind so clearly and so often, it seemed as though they had been together only the day before.

"I'm fine. How are you?"

He sighed and didn't answer. "Are you fine, Raphaella? I mean really . . ." She nodded this time, wondering why he hadn't answered when she asked him how he was. Wasn't he happier. Hadn't he found someone to replace her? Wasn't that why she had released him? Surely her sacrifice had instantly borne fruit. "I still don't understand why you did it." He looked at her bluntly, showing no inclination to leave. He had waited five months to confront her. He wouldn't have left now if they'd dragged him away.

"I told you. We're too different."

"Are we? Two different worlds, is that it?" He sounded bitter. "Who told you that? Your father? Or someone else? One of your cousins in Spain?"

No, she wanted to tell him, *your sister fixed it for us. Your sister, and my father with his goddamn surveillance and threats to tell John Henry, whether it killed him or not . . . that, and my conscience. I want you to have the babies that I'll never have . . .*

"No. No one told me to do it. I just knew it was the right thing to do."

Oh, really? Don't you think we might have discussed it. You know, like grown-ups. Where I come from, people discuss things before they make major decisions that affect other people's lives."

She forced herself to look at him coldly. "It was beginning to affect my husband, Alex."

"Was it? Strange that you only noticed that when you were six thousand miles away from him in Spain."

She looked at him pleadingly then, the agony of the past five months beginning to show in her eyes. He had already noticed how much thinner her face was, how dark were the circles beneath the eyes, how frail were her hands. "Why are you doing this now, Alex?"

"Because you never gave me the chance to in July." He had called her four or five times in San Francisco, and she had refused to take the calls. "Didn't you know what that letter would do to me? Did you think of that at all?" And suddenly, as she saw his face, she understood better. First Rachel had left him, giving him no chance to win against an invisible opponent, a hundred-thousand-dollar-a-year job in New York. And then Raphaella had done almost the same thing, flaunting John Henry and their "differences" as an excuse to walk out. Suddenly she saw it all differently and she ached at what she saw in his eyes. Beneath his piercing gaze she dropped her eyes now and touched the sand with one long thin hand.

"I'm sorry . . . oh, God . . . I'm so sorry . . ." She looked up at him then and there were tears in her eyes. And the pain he saw there brought him to his knees beside her on the sand.

"Do you have any idea how much I love you?"

She turned her head away then and put up a hand as though to stop him from speaking, whispering softly, "Alex, don't . . ." But he took the hand in his own and then with his other hand brought her face back until she looked at him again.

"Did you hear me? I love you. I did then, and I do now, and I always will. And maybe I don't understand you, maybe there are differences between us, but I can learn to understand those differences better, Raphaella. I can if you give me the chance."

"But why? Why only a half life with me when you can have a whole one with someone else?"

"Is that why you did it?" At times he had thought so, but he had never been able to understand why she had severed the tie so quickly, so bluntly. It had to be more than just that.

"Partly." She answered him honestly now, her eyes looked in his. "I wanted you to have more."

"All I wanted was you." And then he spoke more softly. "That's all I want now." But she shook her head slowly in answer.

"You can't have that." And then after a long pause, "It's not right."

"Why not, dammit?" There was fire in his eyes when he asked the question. "Why? Because of your husband? How can you give up all that you are for a man who is almost dead, for a man who, from what you yourself have told me, has always wanted your happiness, and would probably love you enough to set you free if he could?"

Alex knew John Henry had in a sense set Raphaella free already. But he couldn't tell Raphaella of that meeting. Her face bore witness to the terrible strain under which she was suffering. To add to that, to tell her that John Henry knew of their relationship, was unthinkable.

But Raphaella wouldn't listen. "That wasn't the deal I made. For better or worse . . . in sickness and in health . . . until death do us part. Not boredom, not strokes, not Alex . . . I can't let any of that hinder my obligations."

"Damn your obligations." He exploded and Raphaella looked shocked and shook her head.

"No, if I don't honour what I owe him, he'll die. I know that now. My father told me that this summer and he was right. He's barely hanging on now, for God's sake."

"But that has nothing to do with you, dammit, don't you see that? Are you going to let your father run your life too? Are you going to be pushed around by your 'duties' and 'obligations' and your sense of noblesse oblige? What about *you*, Raphaella? What about what *you* want? Do you ever allow yourself to think of that?" The truth was that she tried not to think of it. Not anymore.

"You don't understand, Alex." She spoke so softly that he could barely hear her in the wind. He sat next to her on the log, their bodies so close that it made Raphaella shiver.